Poems To Make You Smile

Steven Harris

Presentation by *BookLeaf Publishing*

Web: www.bookleafpub.com

E-mail: info@bookleafpub.com

ISBN:9789358318685

First edition 2024

DEDICATION

Dedicated to my family who always encouraged me to bring out my more creative side.

Guilty Pleasures

I met a famous, three-star chef
And asked his guilty pleasure.
He wouldn't say a thing at all
Until I got his measure.
Then he opened up to me
And said with some remorse,
"It's a fish finger sandwich
With lots of tartare sauce."

I saw a top barista
And asked her the same question.
Unimpressed and stern of face,
She baulked at the suggestion.
But we continued talking
Until she said, "It's true.
I love a cup of builder's tea,
One sugar, sometimes two."

A literary critic
Seemed to think it was a crime,
When I enquired what he did
To make the most of his spare time.
Then he looked me in the eye,
Replied in a voice so solemn,
"I buy one of the tabloids
And read the gossip column."

A well-known opera singer
Refused to give details
And tell her little secret,
As she practised all her scales.
But once she'd lightened up a bit
And wasn't quite so miffed,
She finally admitted
That she loved Taylor Swift.

Christmas Lunch

It's Christmas Day and so we eat
A turkey full of stuffing.
We all pretend we like it,
Of course we're really bluffing.

If we opened up and told the truth,
I'm sure that we would find
A preference for other foods
And turkeys wouldn't mind!

A side of beef would go down well
With parsnips, mash and peas.
And for our vegetarians,
Some grilled halloumi cheese.

But what about a leg of lamb
With mint sauce on the side?
And lovely thick, dark gravy
Liberally applied.

Of course, we could go right off piste
'Cos we know nothing beats a
Delicious, thin crust, round and red,
Oven-fired pizza!

The Wind

I've had a very tiring day.
I want to sleep in bed,
But squally gusts and rustling leaves
Are doing in my head.

The wind is really picking up,
It's turning to a gale.
It wants to batter down the trees.
I hope that they prevail.

It whistles through the window frame,
The one that needs repair.
It blows the curtains back and forth,
And rocks the rocking chair.

It presses forward to the hall.
I hear it start to roar.
It rams into a painting that
Then crashes to the floor.

So, then it hurtles down the stairs
To set off the alarm.
And next into the kitchen, where
It really does some harm.

The pots and pans are thrown around,
The tea and coffee fall.
My apples, oranges and pears
Are slammed into the wall.

Eventually it settles down
And stillness soon takes hold.
The wind has taken all the heat
And left the house so cold.

But finally I'm left in peace,
There's silence all around.
I curl up tight beneath the sheets
To slumber safe and sound.

Memories Of A DVD Video Game

Fourth shelf up on the right,
Plastic wrapping glistening in the fluorescent
light of the shop.
There it is,
My entertainment for the Christmas holidays.
The best game ever!

Back at home,
I slip the shiny disk into the drive.
A few clicks later and it's off to the races.

The adrenalin rush as I overtake time and again,
Whizzing past the cartoon, cheering crowd.
Over a bump, round a corner, through a tunnel,
Turbo boost on as I rush into the lead.

Yes! Just one lap to go.

Then I'm off the track
And into oblivion.
Time to go again.

This Christmas is going to be so much fun!

The Seasons At School

As September marches into October,
Uniforms at school turn into grey.
The duffle coat is back in season.
Underfoot, the ground is soaking.
Moody teachers shout, "Keep off the grass!"
Nobody takes any notice.

When December comes upon us,
Ice leaves the ground a sugary white.
Noise is dampened by the heavy air.
Teachers come into the playground.
Every child hears the bell for end of break.
Regardless, they keep on playing.

Soon February succumbs to March.
Postcard daffodils burst out in yellow.
Rain means lunchtime in the classroom.
Inside, the children are just bored,
No chance to expend unused energy.
Going to be a trying afternoon!

So we reach the middle of July.
Utter joy pervades under skies of blue.
Maths, English and other exams are over.
Meanwhile, kids enjoy the sunshine.
Even the teachers put on a smile,
Relaxed before the long holiday.

Video Assistant Referee

The TMO in rugby
Is always in control.
The third umpire in cricket
Knows how to play the role.
So why is VAR in football
Such a dreadful mess?
Lots of bad decisions
Mean they get an awful press.

Is it the subjectivity
Of what deserves a red -
Or when to give a penalty
Or wave play on instead?
Is it that they just don't show
The reason for each decision?
If no one knows what's going on
That just adds to the derision.

And when we hear the audio
Days after the event.
It sounds like teenage banter.
So, of course, fans want to vent.
"They're just a bunch of amateurs,"
Is the inevitable cry.
"We need a group of experts
On whom we can rely."

They say that poor decisions
Even out across the season.
But some teams seem to come off worse
And there isn't a good reason.
So come on P.G.M.O.L.,
You need to up your game.
Give us more consistency,
Then you won't get the blame.

Post-COVID Summer

The weather's fab,
We've had our jab.
It's time to make some hay.
"The sun is out,"
I hear you shout,
"Let's go out for the day."

A choice to make,
Which road to take?
Agreement we must reach.
A city tour,
A picnic or
A walk along the beach?

No matter which,
There'll be a hitch.
It always happens so.
A faulty train,
Un-forecast rain,
But why I just don't know.

It seems a shame
And rather lame
To stay at home instead.
A barbecue
Will do us too
On the patio that we laid.

It's all good news
To dodge the queues
That build up everywhere.
Some golden sun
And garden fun,
The good times back to share.

The Lunchbox

What's for lunch this sunny day?
What did my mother make?
Perhaps a sandwich made with meat
And a piece of chocolate cake.

I'm opening the lid right now,
The saliva starts to trickle.
Oh, no! The same as yesterday,
It's ham and cheese and pickle!

Fractions

When I have to calculate fractions,
I can never remember the rule.
Which is the number that goes on the top?
It makes me feel such a fool.

So, I'll leave them for the time being
And come back a little later.
For then I will have remembered
That it is the numerator.

Geography

Geography lost its attraction,
When I went on a trek to a field.
It was cold and the wind kept on blowing,
My umbrella, not much of a shield.

So, I'm giving it up after summer
For a subject that's always inside.
Maybe History, Spanish or Woodwork.
I have until autumn to decide.

Feeding Time At The Zoo

It's time for a change in their diet.
The animals have gone very quiet.
They're all in a mood,
So they'll get better food
Before it turns into a riot.

For the mice we'll get rice,
For the snakes, chocolate cakes.
The hippopotami will have low fat salami.
The lions will eat bigger pieces of meat.
The great crocodiles will have nothing but
smiles,
When we give them a chunk of casseroled
skunk.

But what shall we choose
For the sad kangaroos?
Perhaps they will learn to like toast.
With butter or jam
Or a nice slice of ham,
I wonder which they'll like the most.

Rain Damage

The rain came through the roof one night.
It made an awful mess.
The matter caught me unawares
And led to untold stress.

The water seeped into the beams
That kept the roof aloft.
They lost control of all that weight -
The joints had gone too soft.

I heard the creaking overhead
And looked up with a frown.
Instinctively I knew the house
Would all come crashing down.

I jumped out of my cosy bed
Then hurtled down the stair.
I thought I wouldn't make it out
And blurted out a prayer.

But fate was kind to me that night,
As I sat on the lawn.
The structure didn't all collapse,
It still held come the dawn.

It's true the roof had fallen in,
But not punched through the floor.
The upstairs seemed to be intact.
I couldn't ask for more.

I had to move out while the roof
Repair was underway.
At least the loss adjuster said
I didn't have to pay.

But all is well that does end well
And I am back at home.
My rooftop's had a redesign,
It's now a silver dome.

Christmas Left-Overs

We've so much left on Boxing Day,
Mum won't let it go to waste.
And thinking back a year ago,
It's the same problem that we faced.

Turkey omelette for our breakfast.
Turkey sandwich for our lunch.
And turkey curry for our dinner?
Well, at least, that's just a hunch.

I don't know why she doesn't see
A chicken would suffice.
It's perfect for the four of us
And wouldn't cost the price.

So, next year I'll remind her
That turkey's off the menu.
And if she can't agree to this,
We'll find another venue!

Music In The Classroom

Noise blurting from trumpets and trombones.

Kids whacking drums
and letting sticks crash to the floor,
before crunching them under their feet.

Grade 1 violins scratch your eardrums,
While cymbals rip through your brain.

Then a flute dances lightly over the desks
And the graceful harp gently restores order.

A saxophone mellows everyone into submission.
As calm descends,
It's the end of the lesson.

A triangle tip-toes the children out of the room.

The Origin Of Chocolate

Chocolate came from Mexico
Or so we all believed,
But evidence is gathering
That we have been deceived.

The Spaniards met the Aztecs
And were served a bitter drink,
Made from the cacao bean,
Called chocolatl – or so that's what we think.

They claimed they brought it home with them
And sugared it to taste.
So began the story of
The greatest food the world has ever faced.

It all seems very plausible,
But one thing isn't right.
If cacao was just so valuable,
Why did the Aztecs give it up without a fight?

Archaeology's now showing us
What was really so,
That chocolatl had spread across the world
Millennia ago.

In ancient caves near Burnley
Are handprints made in brown.
All had thought they were ochre,
Abundant round the town.

But now they're tested chemically
And scientists are rattled.
Not the well-known pigment,
But clearly chocolatl.

In the Khorat Plateau of Thailand
There's a bronze age artefact,
An amphora of the brown stuff
Still perfectly intact.

A recent dig in Istanbul,
From the times of a Roman battle,
Shows the pots and pans of the army
Coated in chocolatl.

We'll never know who made it first,
But does it really matter?
We took a bitter, spicy drink
And made it so much better.

By sweetening and adding milk,
We've got the perfect food.
However you are feeling,
It will lighten up your mood.

Aftermath At The Zoo

The animal diet worked well.
They no longer want to rebel.
"With a bit of a rest,
They'll be back to their best,"
Said the zookeeper, "Yes, I can tell."

For the mice, they are nice
And the snakes lost the shakes.
The hippopotami, they love their umami.
The lions are calm, so they'll do no one harm.
The head crocodile is not volatile
And his family have dined, so they're all feeling
fine.

For the sad kangaroos,
We've got rid of the blues,
For it seems they are partial to toast.
But we'd never have guessed
That they like it the best
With carrots and peas and a roast.

The Tight-Head Prop

His playground is the scrum or rolling maul.
He doesn't care about his face at all.
His mangled nose and cauliflower ear
Show he's a player that has no fear.

A tree-trunk neck from hours in the gym.
A chest that is the antonym of slim.
With thighs and calves that put us all to shame,
Just so he can play the splendid game.

I speak of course about the tight-head prop,
The beast that very few can stop.
He crashes into all who dare come by,
From time to time scratching at an opponent's
eye!

And if you ask how he came to lose his teeth,
He'll smile a toothless grin, no hint of grief.
"A punch because their scrum was in reverse,
But their loose-head came off so much worse!"

Vampire

When a vampire's out in the night
And he's right in the mood for a bite.
He remembers his system
To select a poor victim
And ambush before it gets light.

Now his charms, so it's commonly written
Will ensure that you're utterly smitten.
You will lose your direction
And show him affection,
Before finally ending up bitten.

So it's wise to go out with protection.
Garlic is my predilection.
But a cross wouldn't hurt you,
It's surely a virtue
If you don't want to be his selection.

Sunny Day By The Sea

As sunlight fills an azure sky,
There's not a cloud in sight.
This paraglider's so much fun,
As long as I hold tight.

I see the people way below,
Enjoying their day out.
With frisbees, balls and kites galore
Just flying round about.

The wing comes loose. "Oh no!" I shout,
And then I'm dropping fast.
I try to calm my panic, but
My face is all aghast.

Now timing, it is everything,
My landing I judge well.
A bouncy castle saves my life,
I live the tale to tell.

The kids around all look at me.
They'd stopped their joyful play.
I rise a little shaken up
And go on with my day.

I need to find a quiet place
And sit awhile alone.
Reflect upon my fortune with
An ice-cream in a cone.

Then after that I take a walk
Along the golden beach.
The sand gets in between my toes.
"Be gone!" I do beseech.

I look up to the sky above
With 'gliders all around.
I know that from now on I'll keep
Feet firmly on the ground.

The Greatest

The eternal question,
Who or what is the greatest?
It creates debate,
Brings out our passions,
But rarely do we reach accord.

Bach, Mozart or Beethoven?
Do not go gentle, The road not taken or Shall I
compare thee?
Whatever the topic,
We take our stand
And never budge.

Yet in the world of film
The answer is unequivocal.
"The Princess Bride".

A pirate, a sword fight, a giant
And the cliffs of insanity.
Shrieking eels, rodents of unusual size, the
six-fingered man
And "the machine".
A Spaniard, a sweet princess, a wicked prince
And through it all, true love.

Adventure, revenge, humour,
The best film ever.
There's simply no debate.

Six Haikus

Mobile phones were phones.
Then they were entertainment.
Now they are cameras.

"The beautiful game"
Is just twenty-two people
Kicking a football.

What is gravity?
It is not really a force,
But curved space and time.

Classical music
Is certainly not boring.
Just listen to Bach.

Being the adult,
When others act like children,
Can be exhausting.

Why write poetry?
Storytelling? Emotion?
Wordplay is just fun.